Silent Frontier
Icons of Montana's Early Settlement

new photographs by Richard S. Buswell

To the Juniata College Museum of Art
Richard S Buswell
april 9, 2015

Montana Museum of Art & Culture
The University of Montana - Missoula

ACKNOWLEDGMENTS

My sincerest thanks to Maggie Mudd, not only for her wonderful written introduction to this book, but also for her friendship and artistic nurturing over the twelve years that we have worked together. My deepest thanks also to Annick Smith, film maker, author and co-editor of the *Last Best Place*, for her elegant and insightful contribution to this book. David Earhart of the Montana Museum of Art & Culture has been of immeasurable help in bringing this book to fruition, as has the staff at UM Printing & Graphic Services, particularly Tim Lindeborg, Neal Wiegert and Ken Price.   *-R.S.B.*

Research and Economic Development Series, Number 3
Office of Research and Economic Development, The University of Montana

Printed by The University of Montana Printing & Graphic Services
First Printing

Distributor: Farcountry Press

Inside paper: Xpedx LX Velvet 100 lb. book. Acid Free.

Mapping Silent Frontiers

The Montana Museum of Art and Culture enjoys a long relationship with Dr. Richard Buswell of Helena. The first museum to exhibit Buswell's work in a one-person show, he was introduced to Montana audiences through the prescient selection of former curator Dennis Kern in 1991. The Museum has collected and participated in the publication of his images since. More than 80 American museums have followed suit. Now in 2002, a new exhibit will be produced and seen by audiences inside and outside Montana. The reasons are obvious.

Richard Buswell represents an artistic approach to photography that reflects not only his personal aesthetic vision but also the healing he has provided in his chosen profession. And by drawing upon early settlement sites as subject matter Buswell participates in the history of Montana. Not unlike those whose impulses forged the story of his home state, he pioneers a journey of discovery into Montana's past.

The marriage of frontier history and scientific discipline is easily enough bound. But it is Buswell's sensitivity to the meaning of memory that elevates his photographic pursuit of thirty-one years to the level of cultural history. Richard Buswell does not merely catalog a collection of artifacts; he interprets them as signposts on a map of western American psychic terrain.

The American West has been called the last great frontier, but that designation often refers to a physical reality. The deeper fact is, what we behold on our western horizon defines a fragile promise. For the edge or outer margin of American experience, represented by the vast reaches of its empty western quarter, is more than physical. It is a frontier of turf, grass and rocky slope, but also of hope and longing.

Just as Lewis and Clark were, Buswell is on a discovery expedition. It is not, however, the pen but the ultimate tool of modern optics – that which locks an image in a fragile emulsion on celluloid – that is his medium. Through its split-second timing he redefines places barely revealed by those dauntless Jeffersonians but 200 years ago. As his lens discovers anonymous places in the hillsides of Montana's endless valleys, he writes a different history that reinter-prets them from the vantage point of intervening years and a broader cultural awareness. Buswell chronicles the hopeful exhilaration, often mindless exploration, and very mixed success of countless adventurers who followed Lewis and Clark's footsteps into the boundless western horizon. His photography is thus a pivotal contribution to a mature Montana identity. By harkening back to the early habitation of actual places on Montana's face, he charts a cultural landscape that enriches and redefines an experience that is particularly American.

In seeking the past through the contemplation of its relics and the relentless reclamation of nature against them, Richard Buswell reverently posits an eloquent visual clarification to the American zeitgeist revealed in the chronicle of western discovery. His photographs are excava-tions of a spiritual archaeology. In exquisite clinical frames he examines, not the skin and bones, but the heart and soul, of frontier experience in the American West. Objects abandoned in isolated settlements are specimens, a precious detritus, that focus our attention on the challenge and courage of those who built, celebrated and, ultimately, lost them. In a unique interplay of image, history and meaning he maps an uncharted region punctuated by landmarks that are mute and ghostly witnesses to a story in direct conflict with the prevailing mystique of American adventure.

It is the goal of mapmakers to provide a pathway through uncharted territory in order to blaze a way for others. Historians, too, do much the same by researching records, lists and primary accounts that provide an accurate map of the past. Thus, the meaning of history may be mined, the dross seared away. The highways of memory may, as a result, point to better destinations, or so it is hoped. The missions of mapmaker and historian conflate: both are guardians against loss. They are keepers of the true path. For a bad map, as a distorted history, results in blind alleys and dead ends.

On Richard Buswell's map, image and historical artifact merge in a new metaphysics of the American West. On his map, measuring instruments of lens, hand and heart lead viewers back in time in order that they may better recognize the present. He memorializes landmarks—and those often anonymous settlers who created them—to suggest a way into understanding. Buswell does not care where on a physical map we might find this or that object. He rarely identifies. What matters to him is that we grow in our understanding of the frontier experience represented by the visual information he records and interprets. Buswell's long march across Montana's rugged face is scientific in scope and historic in breadth. But its contribution to a deeper understanding of our state's frontier history, and our ability to mine its meaning, flows from the art through which he charts it.

A spirit of artistic and historic discovery has impelled Buswell to continue his youthful ghost town treasure hunts for thirty-one years. Like earlier explorers, his journals, maps and records provide a resource that conveys an understanding of, not just where he has been, but what he has found. His photographs are akin to scientific records and, like all such research, they suggest deeper understanding. It is more than what we learn about where Buswell has been that matters, for his images are the oeuvre of an impeccable artist. His passion is to reveal what the seen world means.

Visual artists, like mapmakers and historians, provide pathways through the mysterious territory of human experience. Their aim is to unwrap the seen world in order to reamalgamate reality and to show a way through it. Their goal is to expand our understanding of human experience. And their specific ability to do so derives its strength from the level of an individual artist's skill. In Buswell's case the aesthetic choice of the silver selenide gelatin print rejects the evanescence of digital, video and color image. Its archival suitability to the austere and weathered relics he records is best explained by the artist: "If we had to depend on color to record our past, there would be nothing left to remember." This sophisticated palette enhances the presence of ghostly found objects as no other can.

The art of the American West has long suffered from an obsessive mythologizing. The West in this mindset was "won." Western landscape was seen as a battleground for a mythic war with Native and nature. Florid visual accounts of bloody skirmishes often justified exploitation at the expense of conscience. Buswell's poignant, elegiac art is a powerful conduit that connects us to another frontier where silence shouts profundity and abandoned objects refute triumphalisms. What is manifest here is a different destiny. Buswell cautions us that perhaps the West was, in truth, never really won.

Western landscape can be relentlessly formidable. Jagged peaks of insurmountable elevation do not invite. They confront. Dark woods, overgrown with forage, hide the stereotypical cunning cat and growling grizzly. Waves of grain beat against the land in vast armies of directional deceit in which one's way is easily lost. Such places can make for a lonely life. They demand a survivor's clarity, surefootedness and unwavering reverence for the magnitude of what is beyond the self. One lives here a life against nature. The reminders are writ large and loud. It is a situation that demands heightened vigilance.

Richard Buswell's photographs record the price of not paying careful attention to this reality. The theme of nature's reclamation inheres in every image. Like all map makers he knows that river banks shift, forests encroach and erosion relentlessly redefines contours, carving the land like soft sand on a tidal shore. His message, whether encased in dusty beauty or brilliant western light, is this: the silence of the frontier is a testimony. The map is never finished. What moves through is destined to perish. Only the way, the passage, matters. What remains is a mere teasing memory of that experience, however sacred or misguided.

Buswell's concern is that of the good doctor, prescribing what is not only palliative, but what may, in fact, save our lives. His stunning photographic alchemy reminds us that physical frontiers are fickle. How we choose to live, our attitudes, our actions create the landmarks on a more important map, that of the frontier within. This frontier pronounces itself in the present. It is an enduring, hidden, fertile territory, the only and ever new land where the human voice may be found. It is the domain of visionaries—philosophers, poets and artists. In a sense, Buswell's choice encompasses all three. His impulse to record, "before we are all gone," presents a poignant legacy at once revelatory and restorative. It is a legacy that, without his voice, is bound to endless silence.

Maggie Mudd
Director, Montana Museum of Art & Culture, 1997-2002

What We Leave Behind

More often than not, the things we leave behind carry more weight than what we take with us. Every deserted object, animate or not, is loaded with memory, promise, and loss. Even when senility cuts down short-term memories and old people no longer recognize their children, the stricken mind recalls some long-ago doll or fishing rod, the iron-framed bed in Mama's room, a haymow where barn owls would scare the beJesus out of you, yellow-eyed and white as ghosts.

The images Richard Buswell records as he searches Montana's overgrown homesteads, mines, mills, and settlements are not mere records of ruin, but painstaking efforts to capture the essence of transformation—lives become artifacts. At the crossroads where archaeology meets art, he photographs the effects of erosion on structures of wood and metal, and the slow patient decay of personal possessions: a glue pot, a birdcage, Chinese lanterns. What sets Buswell apart from a host of amateurs shooting old log barns is the sense of life found in the cracks. He captures not only the vessel, but the human touch that held it. And there's a spiritual quality to many of his photos—the cathedral light, for instance, contained in a broken-down silo. These found images are strong in their clarity. They avoid the postcard clichés of nostalgia yet evoke stories that also lie tangled under the weeds.

Buswell knows that stories are embedded within the artifacts of history, what he calls "the silent frontier." And there's a spark, a whisper, or call perhaps akin to the signal a prey animal sends to her predator—"choose me"—that draws his eye toward one object and not another, a kind of energy released through art. Sometimes, he says, he feels a presence looking over his shoulder, "a strong, emotional feeling that someone's there with me when I take a picture. It's a recurrent, spiritual feeling. Eerie. Scary."

This is not surprising, for ghosts inhabit a ghost town, at least their stories do, and Buswell's pictures evoke stories. When I contemplate his cobwebbed beer bottles in a defunct brewery, I see mouths—mouths open and waiting like baby birds; and the moldering cards, the ten of spades, the deuce of clubs, flung helter-skelter on a gaming table was surely the hand of a loser. Deep in the tunnel whose stones are returning to earth, I imagine a miner yearning for the sun; and bouncing astride the sunlit buggy seat pictured so abstractly you've got to be told what it is, I see a young woman with an ample fanny who dreams of running to town for good!

There is an isolate beauty in the way nature inhabits what people have left behind, and that beauty is its own story: white rings under the eaves of a deserted house left by the mud nests of departed swallows; dry and rotting leaves piled high on a pantry shelf, taking the place of canned tomatoes in Mason jars; grass growing on a fallen sod roof that opens to clouds you might think are mountains. The key to such pictures is the juxtaposition of decay and rebirth. The artist does not decry the "machine in the garden," but celebrates the "garden in the machine." My favorite is a sharply focused shot of delicate serrated leaves, alive and luminous, which rise from the coiled springs of an old mattress.

Leaves and grass, however, are the only living things in Buswell's collection. He photographs faces, but they are dusty, decapitated mannequin heads, mustached, bright-eyed bewigged, and smiling—spookier than Barbara Walters in their perpetual youth. We also see pictures of pictures plastered onto walls: newsprint photos of the Czar's daughters layered like a collage on weathered wood; turn-of-the century society-page ladies who glance sideways from under swatches of flowery wallpaper; a pen-and-ink drawing of a talking man who seems to be courting a demure and pretty woman. This illustration bears the title "LIFE," and is overlain with scraps of newsprint, penciled numbers, and nail holes. The caption says,

Advice to the Mentally Feeble
KEEP THE MOUTH CLOSED

Finally, I smile. There is irony in Buswell's studies, but little humor, and no color. Many of the photographs are cool, like jazz is cool, veering toward abstraction. These are his most recent works, and in them design belies content. The photographer steps back to avoid sentimentality, then focuses in. Patterns of knots inherent in a panel of hand-milled siding are seen to be animate forms—nudes reminiscent of a Henry Moore sculpture—when the wood becomes nonfunctional. A swirl of iron teeth in an old dredge pump softens as it rusts, mocking the uses it was put to. A clutch of coffee pots viewed from the top becomes a composition of circles and bars, and the drum of a player piano in macro-closeup reveals a syncopated pattern reminiscent of Mondrian's "Broadway Boogie Woogie."

In some of his most powerful images, the impulse goes beyond abstraction and toward what he calls reverence. Buswell shoots his frontier artifacts as if they were religious icons, in a bath of light. He surrounds them with dense black emptiness. There are stairs going nowhere, window frames in skeleton walls, a tunnel that drips stalactites, rooftop shakes embroidered with moss, burlap curtains where birds drop their droppings. Such images are eloquent and alive. The lady of the house is gone, but her breath moves the curtains. Children's voices echo in bunchgrass. Sky is all that the silo holds. The dredge pump has emptied the river of gold.

ॐ

Part memory, part eulogy, part celebration, even the most abstract of Buswell's photos depict life reinventing itself. Which is only to be expected, given Buswell's workday profession, for the photographer is a fulltime practicing physician, an allergist. He is familiar with death. And he knows how decay works. But healing is his highest craft and preservation of life is his calling.

The doctor is a fourth-generation Montanan, born in Helena and raised on what he calls a "hobby ranch" near Fort Harrison. One maternal great-grandfather was a coal-miner in Gilt Edge, and his maternal grandfather drove a stagecoach between Lewistown and Roy. His parents, Virginia and Howard, were ghost-town aficionados, and they took their only child with them on weekends, the father searching for minerals, the mother digging in dumps for bottles tinged blue with age.

"My dad was an amateur geologist," he says, "and my earliest memories are camping out in ghost towns. We had this '49 Dodge pickup that Dad converted into a camper, and we'd roast marshmallows on willow sticks over a campfire, then we'd spread our sleeping bags all tucked together in the truck bed."

As a student at Helena High School, Richard served as a photographer for student publications. On one occasion, he went down into the Franklin Mine in the Scratchgravel Hills to photograph miners under the earth. His camera was a Brownie with a flash attachment. The pictures were published in the *Helena Independent Record*, and young Richard received $25 in payment. That's when photography became real to him, a possible calling. But the call of medicine was stronger.

The boy majored in biology at Carroll College, graduating *magna cum laude*. He went to medical school in Oregon, served his residency in Colorado, and then went off to study leukemia and lymphoma at the National Institutes of Health. But in 1971, while in Bethesda, Maryland, Buswell bought his first good camera, a 35mm Nikkormat with a 50mm lens. That fall and on subsequent vacations, he made pilgrimages to the ghost towns of his childhood and began what would become at first a hobby, then a passion, and finally what he describes as "a consumption, if you will."

Buswell still uses his original Nikkormat equipment, now more than 30 years old. He works with a standard 50mm lens, a wide-angle 24mm lens, a macro lens for extreme close-ups, and a zoom lens. He prefers fine-grained black and white films, sets up a tripod for every shot, and uses a hand-held light meter. To get the detailed images so crucial to his vision, he often tries out a variety of timed exposures, but that's as fancy as it gets. The rules of his game are simplicity and portability.

Finding places and artifacts to photograph is more tricky, and depends on research. One source is books. Buswell's interest in Montana history was nurtured by his father, and over many years he has collected a home library about ghost towns, mining, geology, and frontier settlers. But the familiar public places recorded in books are only part of the silent frontier. Many sites are private and unpublished.

"I've got lots of patients," he says, "and word gets around." Patients and friends often direct him to secret troves, and when he hears a promising lead, the meticulous Buswell notes it on a master list that tells him where he's been, and when, and how much of the territory has been explored.

The hunt begins when spring snow melt permits access. Almost every weekend from Easter to Thanksgiving Buswell says goodbye to his doctor self and takes his photographer self out on the prowl. Although he'd go with his father occasionally, when his father was alive, and sometimes takes his teen-age son or one of his two older daughters, he usually goes alone. "I like to be alone" he says. "There's no pressure, except to see. And being alone offers me the occasion to absorb the spirituality of a place."

Each season Buswell chooses certain areas and explores them in depth. Among them was the Stanford region last summer. Maybe somewhere in eastern Montana next year (so far, his focus has been on western parts of the state). Virginia City is always a rich standby. Beyond its tourist attractions are back rooms full of riches. Sheds jammed with artifacts. "I never know what I'm looking for until I see it," he says. "I try to find something I've never seen before." This means that most days the doctor comes home with no newly-exposed negatives.

Winter is printing time and Buswell hunkers down at his Helena home during weekends, passing the dark days in his darkroom. He has studied the printing techniques of famous photographers, especially the archival methods of Ansel Adams. Printing is an exacting art and, trained in scientific methods, the doctor experiments with burning and dodging, different developing solutions, papers, and paper contrasts. Consistent with scientific practice, he keeps notes on the methods he used to make the prints he considers most successful.

CR

Artistic success demands exposure, and Buswell has been quite successful in promoting and selling his work. Tall, elegant, quiet-spoken, he has the kind of professional demeanor that seems worthy of attention. All he has to do is make contact. The work speaks for itself.

As a result, his photographs have been acquired by many notable national museums such as the Museum of Fine Arts, Boston; the Smithsonian Institution's National Museum of American History; the Library of Congress; Harvard University's Fogg Art Museum; and the art museums of Seattle, Denver, Portland, Detroit, Baltimore, New Orleans, Brooklyn, to name only a handful. You will also find Buswell's work in western collections such as the Buffalo Bill Historical Center in Cody, Wyoming, Spokane's Cheney Cowles Museum, and Montana's State Historical Society and C.M. Russell Museum. And he is increasingly the subject of one-man exhibits throughout the West.

This is an amazing achievement for a self-taught, part-time photographer from the outback in Montana. Although he names no single photographer as a guiding influence or model, Buswell's artistic inspiration has come from such visual artists as Charles Burchfield, Andrew Wyeth, Georgia O'Keefe and Edward Hooper. He is drawn to the sense of abandonment in Hooper's paintings, and to the western-inspired light, the clarity and the intensity of O'Keefe.

Perhaps Richard Buswell is reaching national prominence because of the architectural quality of his vision, its purity and sense of design. Or maybe the implied stories inherent in the objects he portrays give his images power. Or, as he is likely to say, it's his reverence for abandoned places—an "iconic reverence" for artifacts that represent life.

Real icons, of course, are religious expressions. Secretive and inscrutable, icons must be contemplated, not understood. They are as close to an art of silence as art can be—yet, paradoxically, although ionic artists were usually anonymous, there is a great arrogance in their work, for these artists were attempting to create perfection and immortality. Iconic artists excite us because they hope to make permanent that which is most mutable. A face. A life. A spirit. But if you believe in icons (and perhaps even if you only believe in art), such images can lead toward the experience of wonder. They cause the viewer to marvel. As one medieval Serbian once wrote about an icon of the saints Sava and Simeon, "I marvel at you and rejoice as though you were alive."

And this is what Buswell's most overtly spiritual photographs attempt. The pictures I'm talking about consist of crosses and lines and circles, almost but not actually abstract, and pointing upward toward the light. There is one called "Rafters," in which beams wrapped in the gleaming metal of newspaper prepress sheets form a cross. And the less obvious "Feeding Trough No. 3," whose wood is weathered like an old hide, sun illuminating the grain, one arm of the cross missing. Then there's the Silo—circular walls rising up a vertical ladder to an explosion of rays at the top—a stained-glass window in a gothic cathedral.

But the most telling iconic image of the collection is, for me, the Medicine Lodge. Here is a human structure that goes back beyond the frontier. It is barely distinguishable from the leaning fir trees behind it, the fallen, decaying limbs on the ground. Shaped like a triangle. Pointing toward the sun. We see tufts of moss on the dried and cracked poles. Lichened rocks form a medicine ring. The light that shines on this pile of stacked sticks is diffuse and brilliant. The image is perfect, the place sacred. We marvel and rejoice.

Annick Smith
Blackfoot Valley, Montana 2002

Print Shop

Newspaper in a Window

PLATE 2

Cabin Interior
PLATE 3

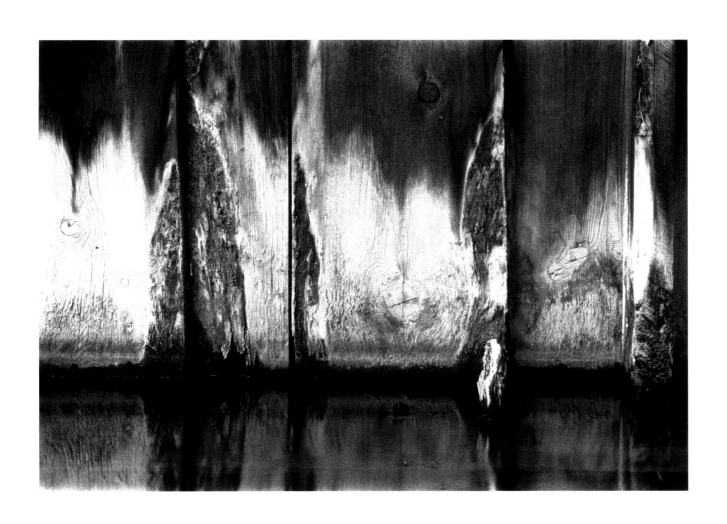

Spring House
PLATE 4

Three Ladies: Newspaper-Wallpaper

PLATE 5

The Czar's Daughters

PLATE 6

Boiler Tubes

PLATE 7

Brickyard Vents

PLATE 8

Where Swallows Lived

PLATE 9

Ceiling
PLATE 10

Medicine Lodge
PLATE 11

Lean-to

PLATE 12

Sod Roof

PLATE 13

Silo

PLATE 14

Chimney

PLATE 15

Stone Chimney

PLATE 16

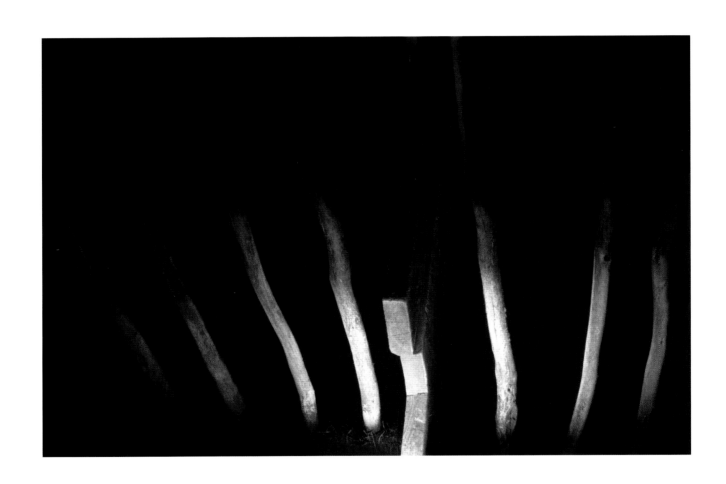

Hay Feeder

PLATE 17

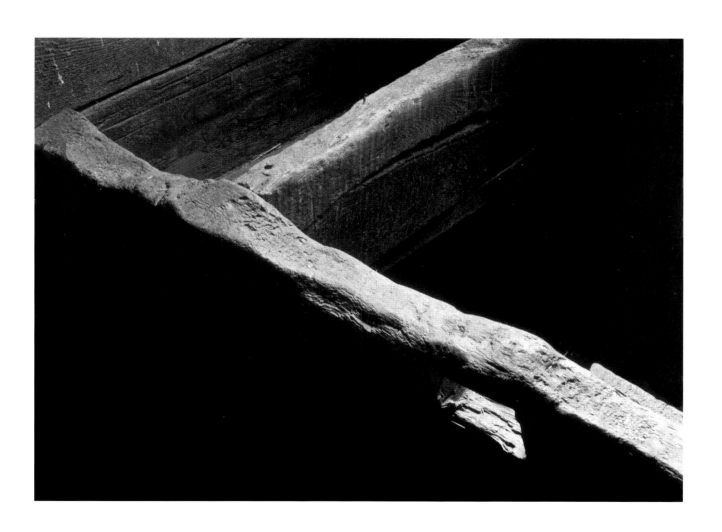

Feeding Trough No. 3

Chinese Lanterns

PLATE 19

Bird Cage

PLATE 20

Mill Boiler, Interior

PLATE 21

Mine Pipes
PLATE 22

Bottles in a Brewery
PLATE 23

Typewriter
PLATE 24

Coffee Pots

PLATE 25

Cards

Chair

PLATE 27

Chair Back

PLATE 28

Blackboard (Juniors 1910)
PLATE 29

Wall Drawing

PLATE 30

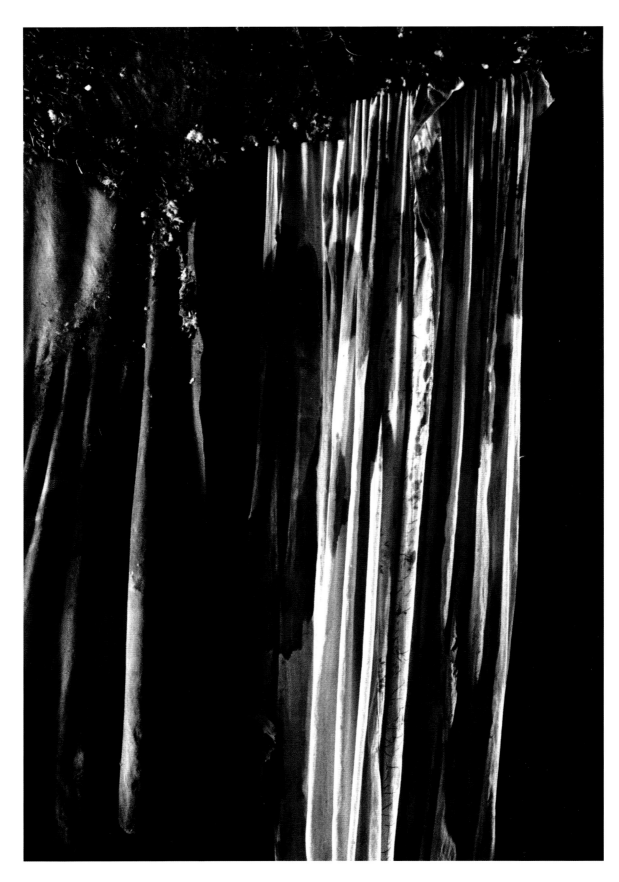

Boudoir

PLATE 31

Burlap Drapes
PLATE 32

Bar Panel

PLATE 33

Water Wheel

PLATE 34

Tram Wheels

PLATE 35

Dredge Pump
PLATE 36

Carriage Seats
PLATE 37

Buggy Seat
PLATE 38

Shelf

PLATE 39

Glue Pot
PLATE 40

Player Piano Drum

PLATE 41

Piano Hammers

PLATE 42

Blacksmith's Tools
PLATE 43

Blacksmith's Window

PLATE 44

Mossy Shingles
PLATE 45

Homestead Ceiling
PLATE 46

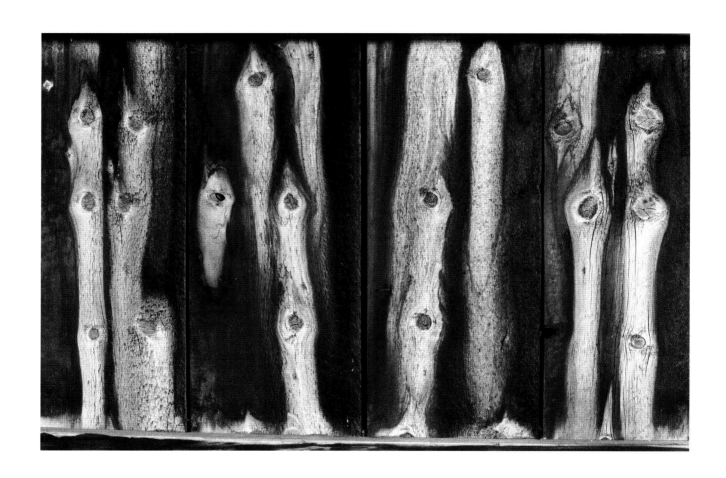

Knots
PLATE 47

Two Knots

PLATE 48

Three Mannequin Heads

PLATE 49

Bone Wagon

PLATE 50

Stuffed Chair
PLATE 51

Bedsprings
PLATE 52

Mill Window
PLATE 53

Missing Floor
PLATE 54

Rafters

PLATE 55

V I T A

RICHARD S. BUSWELL

SOLO EXHIBITIONS

2005   Holter Museum of Art , Helena, Montana (scheduled)

2002-2003   Paris Gibson Square Museum of Art , Great Falls, Montana (scheduled)

2002   Montana Museum of Art and Culture, The University of Montana, Missoula, Montana
Northwest Art Center, Minot State University, Minot, North Dakota
Medicine Hat Museum and Art Gallery, Medicine Hat, Alberta, Canada

2001   Iris and B. Gerald Cantor Art Gallery, College of the Holy Cross, Worcester, Massachusetts
Braithwaite Fine Arts Gallery, Southern Utah University, Cedar City, Utah
Plains Art Museum, Fargo, North Dakota
Hockaday Museum of Art, Kalispell, Montana

2000   Mon-Dak Heritage Center, Sidney, Montana
Emerson/Beall Park Art Center, Bozeman, Montana
Holter Museum of Art, Helena, Montana

1999   Gallery of the BICC Building, Oregon Health Sciences University, Portland, Oregon
Frye Art Museum, Seattle, Washington
Kimball Art Center, Park City, Utah
Arts Chateau, Butte, Montana
Gallery and Museum, The University of Montana-Western, Dillon, Montana

1998   Center for Arts and History, Lewis-Clark State College, Lewiston, Idaho
Copper Village Museum and Arts Center, Anaconda, Montana

1997   Davis Gallery, Department of Art and Pre-Architecture, Idaho State University, Pocatello, Idaho

1996   Department of Fine Arts, Carroll College, Helena, Montana

1993   Western Heritage Center, Billings, Montana
Gallery and Museum, The University of Montana-Western, Dillon, Montana

1992   Holter Museum of Art, Helena, Montana
Museum of Fine Arts, The University of Montana, Missoula, Montana

2002   New Art of the West 8 (National Juried Exhibition), Eiteljorg Museum of American Indians and Western Art, Indianapolis, Indiana

ANA 31 (National Juried Exhibition), Holter Museum of Art, Helena, Montana

Photo National 2002 (National Juried Exhibition, **Juror's Award**), Lancaster Museum of Art, Lancaster, Pennsylvania

7th Annual Photographic Competition/Exhibition, Personal Viewpoints, Photographic Center Northwest, Seattle, Washington

DeCordova Collects: Recent Acquisitions from The Permanent Collection, DeCordova Museum and Sculpture Park, Lincoln, Massachusetts

74th Annual National Juried Exhibition, Art Association of Harrisburg, Harrisburg, Pennsylvania

7th Annual In Focus National Juried Photography Exhibition, Center for Arts and History, Lewis-Clark State College, Lewiston, Idaho

"Views and Visions: Montana Landscape Photography," Museum of the Rockies, Montana State University, Bozeman, Montana

2002 Works on Paper: Recent Drawing, Prints and Photographs (National Juried Exhibition), Union Art Gallery, Louisiana State University, Baton Rouge, Louisiana

17th Annual International Exhibition (Juried), The University of Texas at Tyler, Tyler, Texas

Dishman Competition (National Juried Exhibition), The Dishman Art Gallery, Lamar University, Beaumont, Texas

5th American Print Biennial (National Juried Exhibition), Marsh Art Gallery, University of Richmond Museums, Richmond, Virginia

Positive/Negative 17 (National Juried Exhibition), Slocumb Galleries, East Tennessee State University, Johnson City, Tennessee

Members Showcase 2002, Berkeley Art Center Association, Berkeley, California

23rd Annual Paper in Particular (National Juried Exhibition), Columbia College, Columbia, Missouri

2001   11th Annual Center Awards, Center for Photographic Art, Carmel, California

Light^2: Images from the Photography Collections, Alfred O. Kuhn Library Gallery, University of Maryland, Baltimore County, Baltimore, Maryland

Winter Showcase Invitational, Holter Museum of Art, Helena, Montana

36th Annual Open National, Fine Arts Institute, San Bernardino County Museum, Redlands, California

Art on the Plains, 4th Annual Regional Juried Exhibition (**Juror's Choice Award**), Plains Art Museum, Fargo, North Dakota

Art Equinox 2001: A Regional Survey of Contemporary Art (Regional Juried Exhibition), Paris Gibson Square Museum of Art, Great Falls, Montana

18th Annual National Juried Exhibition, Berkeley Art Center Association, Berkeley, California

6th Annual Photographic Competition Exhibition (National Juried Exhibition), Photographic Center Northwest, Seattle, Washington

18th Annual Lewis-Clark National Juried Exhibition, Center for Arts and History, Lewis-Clark State College, Lewiston, Idaho

2001 National Juried Exhibition, Provincetown Art Association and Museum, Provincetown, Massachusetts

73rd Annual National Juried Exhibition, Art Association of Harrisburg, Harrisburg, Pennsylvania

In Focus National Juried Photography Exhibition, Center for Arts and History, Lewis-Clark State College, Lewiston, Idaho

14th Annual ARTStravaganza (National Juried Exhibition), Hunter Museum of American Art, Chattanooga, Tennessee

7th Annual National Art Exhibition (National Juried Exhibition), St. John's University, Jamaica, New York

16th Annual National Works on Paper (National Juried Exhibition), The University of Texas at Tyler, Tyler, Texas

Current Work 2001 (National Juried Exhibition), Fayetteville State University, Fayetteville, North Carolina

2001 International Juried Show, New Jersey Center for Visual Arts, Summit, New Jersey

Positive/Negative 16 Exhibition (National Juried Exhibition), Slocumb Galleries, East Tennessee State University, Johnson City, Tennessee

22nd Annual Paper in Particular National Juried Exhibition, Columbia College, Columbia, Missouri

2000   35th Annual International Juried Exhibition (**Honorable Mention**), Fine Arts Institute, San Bernardino County Museum, Redlands, California

Winter Showcase Invitational, Holter Museum of Art, Helena, Montana

American Identities: land, people, word, body, spirit, The Art Museum of State University of New York, Potsdam, New York

10th Annual Photography Exhibition (National Juried Exhibition), Maryland Federation of Art, Annapolis, Maryland

Forty Freedoms Exhibition—A Northern Rockies Invitational, Museum of Fine Arts, The University of Montana, Missoula, Montana

3rd Annual Regional Juried Exhibition: Art on the Plains (**Juror's Choice Award**), Plains Art Museum, Fargo, North Dakota

Crosscurrents—A triennial National Juried Exhibition of Contemporary Art, Walter Anderson Museum of Art, Ocean Springs, Mississippi

17th Annual Lewis-Clark National Juried Art Exhibition, Center for Arts and History, Lewis-Clark State College, Lewiston, Idaho

13th Annual ARTStravaganza (National Juried Exhibition), Hunter Museum of American Art, Chattanooga, Tennessee

72nd Annual National Juried Exhibition, Art Association of Harrisburg, Harrisburg, Pennsylvania

In Focus National Juried Photography Exhibition (**Judge's Award**), Center for Arts and History, Lewis-Clark State College, Lewiston, Idaho

23rd Annual Art on Paper National Juried Exhibition, Maryland Federation of Art, Annapolis, Maryland

15th Annual National Works on Paper (National Juried Exhibition), The University of Texas at Taylor, Tyler, Texas

New Photography in the Collection, Art Museum of Missoula, Missoula, Montana

12th Annual National Juried Competition, Truman State University, Kirksville, Missouri

21st Annual Paper in Particular National Juried Exhibition, Columbia College, Columbia, Missouri

Americas 2000 Paper Works (National Juried Exhibition), Minot State University, Minot, North Dakota

1999-2000   Winter Showcase Invitational, Holter Museum of Art, Helena, Montana

1999   Union Art Gallery National Juried Exhibition, Louisiana State University, Baton Rouge, Louisiana

12th Annual ARTStravaganza (National Juried Exhibition, **Juror's Award**), Hunter Museum of American Art, Chattanooga, Tennessee

17th Annual National Juried Exhibition, Alexandria Museum of Art, Alexandria, Louisiana

16th Lewis-Clark National Juried Art Exhibition, Center for Arts and History, Lewis-Clark State College, Lewiston, Idaho

Art Equinox 1999: A Regional Survey of Contemporary Art (Regional Juried Exhibition), Paris Gibson Square Museum of Art, Great Falls, Montana

1999 National Works on Paper (National Juried Exhibition), St. John's University, Jamaica, New York

71st Annual International Juried Exhibition, Art Association of Harrisburg, Harrisburg, Pennsylvania

In Focus (Invitational Photography Exhibition), Center for Arts and History, Lewis-Clark State College, Lewiston, Idaho

Canyon Country Fine Art Competition (National Juried Exhibition), Braithwaite Fine Arts Gallery, Southern Utah University, Cedar City, Utah

Dishman Competition (National Juried Exhibition), The Dishman Art Gallery, Lamar University, Beaumont, Texas

30th National Juried Exhibition, Palm Spring Desert Museum, Palm Springs, California

Greater Midwest International Exhibition XIV (International Juried Exhibition), Central Missouri State University, Warrensburg, Missouri

Paper in Particular '99 National Juried Exhibition, Columbia College, Columbia, Missouri

Positive/Negative 14 Exhibition (National Juried Exhibition), Slocumb Galleries, East Tennessee State University, Johnson City, Tennessee

1998-1999   A Fine and Private Place: Mortality, Monuments and Memories, Denver Art Museum, Denver, Colorado

Collections: Recent Northwest Acquisitions, Tacoma Art Museum, Tacoma, Washington

Annual Exhibition and Auction, Art Museum of Missoula, Missoula, Montana

Winter Showcase Invitational, Holter Museum of Art, Helena, Montana

The Paving of Paradise: A Century of Photographs of the Western Landscape, Seattle Art Museum, Seattle, Washington

1998   33rd Annual International Juried Exhibition, Fine Arts Institute, San Bernardino County Museum, Redlands, California

4th Annual Photographic Competition (National Juried Exhibition), Photographic Center Northwest, Seattle, Washington

Dias de Los Muertos Festival (Regional Juried Exhibition), Hockaday Museum of Art, Kalispell, Montana

16th Annual National Juried Exhibition, Alexandria Museum of Art, Alexandria, Louisiana

15th Lewis-Clark National Juried Art Exhibition, Center for Arts and History, Lewis-Clark State College, Lewiston, Idaho

In Focus (Invitational Photography Exhibition), Center for Arts and History, Lewis-Clark State College, Lewiston, Idaho

11th Annual ARTStravaganza (National Juried Exhibition), Hunter Museum of American Art, Chattanooga, Tennessee

1998 National Juried Exhibition, Provincetown Art Association and Museum, Provincetown, Massachusetts

Montana Interpretations 1998 (Regional Juried Exhibition), Montana Institute of Arts, Butte, Montana

29th National Juried Exhibition (**Honorable Mention**), Palm Springs Desert Museum, Palm Springs, California

4th Annual National Juried Art Exhibition, St. John's University, Jamaica, New York

19th Annual Paper in Particular National Juried Exhibition, Columbia College, Columbia, Missouri

1997   Winter Showcase Invitational, Holter Museum of Art, Helena, Montana

32nd Annual International Juried Exhibition, Fine Arts Institute, San Bernardino County Museum, Redlands, California

ANA 26 (National Juried Exhibition, **Honorable Mention**), Holter Museum of Art, Helena, Montana

Americas 2000 (National Juried Exhibition), Northwest Art Center, Minot State University, Minot, North Dakota

Montana, Myths and Reality, Sutton West Gallery and Center for The Rocky Mountain West of The University of Montana, Missoula, Montana

In Focus (Invitational Photography Exhibition), Center for Arts and History, Lewis-Clark State College, Lewiston, Idaho

Crosscurrents Exhibition (Regional Juried Exhibition), Holter Museum of Art, Helena, Montana

69th Annual International Juried Exhibition, Art Association of Harrisburg, Harrisburg, Pennsylvania

14th Lewis-Clark National Juried Art Exhibition, Center for Arts and History, Lewis-Clark State College, Lewiston, Idaho

Dishman Competition (National Juried Exhibition), The Dishman Art Gallery, Lamar University, Beaumont, Texas

Where Do We Live? Images of House and Home from the Permanent Collection, Art Museum of Missoula, Missoula, Montana

Positive/Negative #12 Exhibition (National Juried Exhibition), Slocumb Galleries, East Tennessee State University, Johnson City, Tennessee

1996   Winter Showcase Invitational, Holter Museum of Art, Helena, Montana

31st Annual International Juried Exhibition, Fine Arts Institute, San Bernardino County Museum, Redlands, California

Kaleidoscope 1996, Department of Fine Arts, Carroll College, Helena, Montana

Magnum Opus IX (International Juried Exhibition), Sacramento Fine Arts Center, Carmichael, California

ANA 25 (National Juried Exhibition), Holter Museum of Art, Helena, Montana

68th Annual International Juried Exhibition, Art Association of Harrisburg, Harrisburg, Pennsylvania
"Jail Exposures" (Two Person Exhibition), Myrna Loy Center, Helena, Montana
27th National Juried Exhibition, Palm Springs Desert Museum, Palm Springs, California
Dishman Competition (National Juried Exhibition), The Dishman Art Gallery, Lamar University, Beaumont, Texas

1995   Winter Showcase Invitational, Holter Museum of Art, Helena, Montana
Kaleidoscope 1995, Department of Fine Arts, Carroll College, Helena, Montana
Annual Exhibition and Auction, Art Museum of Missoula, Missoula, Montana
ANA 24 (National Juried Exhibition), Holter Museum of Art, Helena, Montana
Chautauqua Art Association Galleries, Chautauqua, New York
Texas National '95 (National Juried Exhibition), College of Fine Arts, Stephen F. Austin State University, Nacogdoches, Texas
26th National Juried Exhibition, Palm Springs Desert Museum, Palm Springs, California
North Dakota National Juried Exhibition, Minot Art Gallery, Minot, North Dakota
"Photographing The American West," Paris Gibson Square Museum of Art, Great Falls, Montana

1994   Annual Exhibition and Auction, Missoula Museum of the Arts, Missoula, Montana
The Governor's Culture Foundation, Montana Governor's Mansion, Helena, Montana
"Montana Artists," Idaho Falls Art Council Gallery, Idaho Falls, Idaho
Pacific Northwest Annual (Regional Juried Exhibition), Bellevue Art Museum, Bellevue, Washington
MiniTreasures: Art of the West, Holter Museum of Art, Helena, Montana

1990-1992   "Montana Reflections: Contemporary Photographs—Historic Visions," Museum of the Montana State Historical Society, Helena, Montana

SELECT PUBLIC COLLECTIONS

Museum of Fine Arts, Boston, Massachusetts
Corcoran Gallery of Art, Washington, D.C.
Museum of Fine Arts, Houston, Texas
The Detroit Institute of Arts, Detroit, Michigan
Denver Art Museum, Denver, Colorado
Seattle Art Museum, Seattle, Washington
Baltimore Museum of Art, Baltimore, Maryland
Brooklyn Museum of Art, Brooklyn, New York
Smithsonian Institution, National Museum of American History, Photographic History Collection, Washington, D.C.
Library of Congress, Prints and Photographs Division, Washington, D.C.
Fogg Art Museum, Harvard University, Cambridge, Massachusetts
Yale University Art Collection, New Haven, Connecticut
Nelson-Atkins Museum of Art, Kansas City, Missouri
New Orleans Museum of Art, New Orleans, Louisiana
Worcester Art Museum, Worcester, Massachusetts
Dallas Museum of Art, Dallas, Texas
Chrysler Museum of Art, Norfolk, Virginia
Indianapolis Museum of Art, Indianapolis, Indiana
Portland Art Museum, Portland, Oregon
Cincinnati Art Museum, Cincinnati, Ohio
Columbus Museum of Art, Columbus, Ohio
Rhode Island School of Design Museum of Art, Providence, Rhode Island

Smith College Museum of Art, Northampton, Massachusetts

Herbert F. Johnson Museum of Art, Cornell University, Ithaca, New York

Delaware Art Museum, Wilmington, Delaware

Honolulu Academy of Arts, Honolulu, Hawaii

Orlando Museum of Art, Orlando, Florida

Memphis Brooks Museum of Art, Memphis, Tennessee

Mobile Museum of Art, Mobile, Alabama

The Dayton Art Institute, Dayton, Ohio

Tampa Museum of Art, Tampa, Florida

Butler Institute of American Art, Youngstown, Ohio

Grunwald Center for the Graphic Arts, Armand Hammer Museum of Art and Cultural Center, University of
    California at Los Angeles, Los Angeles, California

Museum of Photographic Arts, San Diego, California

University of Michigan Museum of Art, Ann Arbor, Michigan

Krannert Art Museum and Kinkead Pavilion, University of Illinois at Urbana-Champaign, Champaign, Illinois

Elvehjem Museum of Art, University of Wisconsin-Madison, Madison, Wisconsin

Fred Jones Jr. Museum of Art, University of Oklahoma, Norman, Oklahoma

Rockwell Museum, Corning, New York

The Snite Museum of Art, University of Notre Dame, Notre Dame, Indiana

Palace of the Governors, Museum of New Mexico, Santa Fe, New Mexico

San Antonio Museum of Art, San Antonio, Texas

Springfield Museum of Fine Arts, Springfield, Massachusetts

Frederick R. Weisman Art Museum, University of Minnesota, Minneapolis, Minnesota

Mead Art Museum, Amherst College, Amherst, Massachusetts

Mary and Leigh Block Museum of Art, Northwestern University, Evanston, Illinois

Spencer Museum of Art, The University of Kansas, Lawrence, Kansas

Buffalo Bill Historical Center, Cody, Wyoming

The Montana Museum of Art and Culture, The University of Montana, Missoula, Montana

Holter Museum of Art, Helena, Montana

Museum of the Montana State Historical Society, Helena, Montana

BIBLIOGRAPHY

Major Publications: 1997   *Echoes: A Visual Reflection* (revised and enlarged) Archival Press in association with the Museum of Fine Arts, The University of Montana

         1992   *Echoes: A Visual Reflection*
The University of Montana School of Fine Arts, Missoula, Montana
Catalogue received first place award for the In Plant International
Conference Competition: "In Print '93."

Exhibit Catalogues: 2001   2001 Art Equinox: A Regional Survey of Contemporary Art
Paris Gibson Square Museum of Art

                             Fayetteville State University
Current Work 2001 Exhibition (CD ROM)

         2000   American Identities: land, people, word, body, spirit
The State University of New York College at Potsdam

         1999   Alexandria Museum of Art
17th Annual September Competition (Interactive CD ROM)

                             Art Equinox: A Regional Survey of Contemporary Art
Paris Gibson Square Museum of Art

                             Greater Midwest International Exhibition XIV
Central Missouri State University

                             East Tennessee State University Positive/Negative
14th National Juried Exhibit

         1998   Alexandria Museum of Art
16th Annual September Competition

         1995   Texas National '95 Exhibition

         1994   Missoula Museum of the Arts
Annual Exhibition and Auction